THE
ROLLING
STONES

50 YEARS OF ROCK 'N' ROLL

LIFE BOOKS

MANAGING EDITOR Robert Sullivan

DIRECTOR OF PHOTOGRAPHY
Barbara Baker Burrows

CREATIVE DIRECTOR
Anke Stohlmann

DEPUTY PICTURE EDITOR
Christina Lieberman

COPY EDITORS
Barbara Gogan (Chief),
Don Armstrong, Parlan McGaw

WRITER-REPORTERS
Marilyn Fu (Chief), Michelle DuPré

PHOTO ASSOCIATE Sarah Cates

CONSULTING PICTURE EDITORS
Mimi Murphy (Rome),
Tala Skari (Paris)

EDITORIAL DIRECTOR
Stephen Koepp

EDITORIAL OPERATIONS
Richard K. Prue (Director), Brian
Fellows (Manager), Keith Aurelio,
Charlotte Coco, Kevin Hart, Mert
Kerimoglu, Rosalie Khan, Patricia Koh,
Marco Lau, Brian Mai, Po Fung Ng,
Rudi Papiri, Robert Pizaro, Barry
Pribula, Clara Renauro, Katy Saunders,
Samantha Schwendaman, Hia Tan,
Vaune Trachtman

TIME HOME ENTERTAINMENT

PUBLISHER Richard Fraiman

VICE PRESIDENT, BUSINESS
DEVELOPMENT & STRATEGY
Steven Sandonato

EXECUTIVE DIRECTOR,
MARKETING SERVICES Carol Pittard

EXECUTIVE DIRECTOR, RETAIL &
SPECIAL SALES Tom Mifsud

EXECUTIVE DIRECTOR, NEW
PRODUCT DEVELOPMENT
Peter Harper

DIRECTOR, BOOKAZINE
DEVELOPMENT & MARKETING
Laura Adam

PUBLISHING DIRECTOR Joy Butts

FINANCE DIRECTOR
Glenn Buonocore

ASSISTANT GENERAL COUNSEL
Helen Wan

ASSISTANT DIRECTOR, SPECIAL
SALES Ilene Schreider

BOOK PRODUCTION MANAGER
Suzanne Janso

DESIGN & PREPRESS MANAGER
Anne-Michelle Gallero

BRAND MANAGER Roshni Patel

SPECIAL THANKS: Christine Austin,
Jeremy Biloon, Jim Childs, Susan
Chodakiewicz, Rose Cirrincione,
Jacqueline Fitzgerald, Christine Font,
Jenna Goldberg, Lauren Hall Clark,
Carrie Hertan, Hillary Hirsch, Amy
Mangus, Robert Marasco, Kimberly
Marshall, Amy Migliaccio, Nina Mistry,
Dave Rozzelle, Adriana Tierno,
Alex Voznesenskiy, Vanessa Wu

PAGE 1 Mick Jagger in Paris, 1966.
Photograph by Jean-Marie Périer/
Photo 12/Polaris

PAGES 2–3 Keith Richards in Los
Angeles, 1967. Photograph by Jean-
Marie Périer/Photo 12/Polaris

THESE PAGES Keith's hands,
identifiable by his famous skull ring.
Photograph by Ken Regan/Camera 5

ENDPAPERS Andrew Hawley/Vintage
Concert Poster Buyer Inc. (4); GAB
Archive/Redferns/Getty (7)

THE ROLLING STONES

50 YEARS OF ROCK 'N' ROLL

LONDON, 1964

HAMBURG, GERMANY, 1965

ALTAMONT SPEEDWAY, LIVERMORE, CALIFORNIA, 1969

FIFTH AVENUE, NEW YORK CITY, 1975

ANAHEIM STADIUM, ANAHEIM, CALIFORNIA, 1978

LADIES AND GENTLEMEN: THE ROLLING STONES

What rock 'n' roll bands do not do is reach the top and stay there for 50 years. They do not fill the world's largest arenas every time they announce a new super-tour. They do not leave thrilled thousands screaming just as they did back in the '60s.

Unless, of course, the band is the immortal Rolling Stones.

The Stones were not, as we will soon learn, founded by Mick Jagger and Keith Richards; in fact, neither of the two principal architects of the original "Rollin' Stones" is still alive, nor has been for some time. But Mick and Keith were two of the original Stones back in the spring of 1962, Charlie Watts joined within a matter of months, and those three band-mates are bandmates still as their golden anniversary approaches in 2012. Ronnie

Rock 'n' roll bands come and go. Bands soar to the heights and they crash and burn. Bands disintegrate. Bands break up. Bands reunite. Bands, sometimes with as little as 20 percent of their original DNA, play the oldies circuit—posing as their former selves.

Wood has been a Stone for more than 35 years now. These bare facts are remarkable.

But a rock group is not made interesting or colorful by statistics, no matter how large the number of years or chart-topping hits. The Stones have, down the decades, contrived to make their saga interesting and colorful in a vigorously proactive way that has nothing to do with stats. They were the original bad boys, onstage and off, and bad boys always make for juicy tales to tell (not to mention, great pictures).

Hollywood, were it casting its rock band epic, could not invent a more flamboyant or charismatic frontman than Mick Jagger. When looking for the "incendiary guitarist living life on the edge," the producers could not concoct anything near as riveting as the real-life Keith Richards. Then you throw in the brotherly love-hate relationship that has existed between these two since they were 7-year-olds in a London suburb, the steadying influence of sage Charlie Watts back behind his drum kit, the many children and wives and girlfriends, the backstabbing of band members and managers, the drugs and drug busts, the deaths (inside the band and even in the audience)— and then, oh what the heck, *Pirates of the Caribbean*—and, well: Ladies and gentlemen, we give you the Rolling Stones. Were Shakespeare a contemporary rock-beat writer, this band would be his *King Lear.*

The Stones were always willful in shaping their image, but this commemorative LIFE book is not built on Stones-approved photography. When the Rolling Stones (and

THEN AND NOW: In the photo opposite, from left, Charlie, Keith, Bill Wyman, Mick and Brian Jones. Above: The three who are still Stones—Charlie, Mick and Keith.

the Beatles, who will share a chapter here with their comradely rivals) came on the scene, LIFE was America's pictorial chronicle of what was doing in the world. There are photos here that haven't been published in nearly a half century. Later in the 1960s, '70s, '80s and beyond, intimate behind-the-scenes pictures of the Stones were made— holed up, preparing for a tour, even getting married. The photographers who were granted access were old friends of LIFE, and their images, too, are revisited in our pages. Sometimes an iconic entity like the Rolling Stones can be imagined instantly: Mick leaping, with Keith chugging fiercely behind. But there is so much more to see, as we hope our book will prove.

"This is the life," Keith Richards wrote not long ago, attempting to describe his wonderful memoir. "Believe it or not I haven't forgotten any of it."

Well, believe it or not, it was captured in pictures.

WHO WAS
IAN STEWART?

IN MAY 1967, five years after cofounding the Rolling Stones, Ian "Stu" Stewart is at Olympic Studios in Barnes, in south west London, working on the track "We Love You" with Keith Richards. In his memoir, *Life,* Richards writes that every time he takes the stage with the Stones, he still feels like he is working for Stu.

I f there are several claimants to the title of "fifth Beatle"—the most legitimate being Brian Epstein, though such as Pete Best and Stuart Sutcliffe have worthy cases— there is no doubt as to who was the sixth Rolling Stone in the early days. In fact, the audition in the spring of 1962 that saw Mick Jagger and Keith Richards join Ian Stewart and Brian Jones in forming a new rhythm-and-blues band—a historic meeting now seen by historians and the band itself as the birth of the group—was largely Stu's gig. "To me the Rolling Stones is his band," writes Richards in his memoir. "Without his knowledge and organization . . . we'd be nowhere." It needs be said: Not only Stu's knowledge and organization but also his boogie-woogie piano playing and arranging skills, which pushed the Stones toward their gutbucket rock 'n' roll sound, were vital to their success. If all of this is true, then why is Stewart so relatively anonymous as a Stone? The answer is on these next several pages.

THIS IS WHAT the Rolling Stones once looked like. From left: Brian Jones, Bill Wyman, Charlie Watts, Ian Stewart, Keith Richards and Mick Jagger. Five-sixths of this lineup would become famous, Stewart being the odd man out. And that had everything to do with a man named Andrew Loog Oldham.

ONCE ANDREW OLDHAM was
accepted as the band's manager in 1963,
he determined that the beefy, square-
looking Scotsman Stewart didn't fit the
image he was trying to forge, and also
that six Stones was one too many. He
told Stewart he could continue playing on
records and even onstage in the shadows,
and could continue carting the equip-
ment around in the van he had bought
for the group, but the five faces of the
band would not include his. Richards later
recalled, "I'd probably have said, 'Well,
[expletive] you,' but he said, 'OK, I'll just
drive you around.' That takes a big heart,
but Stu had one of the largest hearts
around." This photograph from 1963
speaks volumes about the relegation of
Ian Stewart.

ABOVE: Stewart in the background in 1964. Opposite, top, from left: Still playing his part in 1973 and in 1971. Bottom: Alongside the man who booted him offstage (Oldham, in shades) in '64. Stewart's contributions to the Stones remained vital for years; his distinctive, driving piano powered hits such as "Honky Tonk Women" and "Brown Sugar," and his opinion on musical matters was as valued as anyone's. "Stu was the one guy we tried to please," said Jagger. "We wanted his approval when we were writing or rehearsing a song." Nevertheless, the Ian Stewart part of the Stones saga is somewhere between poignant and sad—he was the one who got kicked out

IN LATE 1969, Stu, in his work clothes for this particular American tour (this stop is in Los Angeles), carries guitars to the stage. He said rather forlornly, "It seems I'm to wear a white tuxedo. It's going to cost them a bloody fortune to have me play with them, and even more if I have to wear a tux. Cash every night. One thousand dollars. Two thousand with the tux." Despite his "bloody fortune" estimation, this was another cruel thing: When Oldham cut Stu from the lineup, Brian Jones promised the money would continue to be split six ways, but that plan quickly eroded and Stewart became a hired hand—despite Richards's warm protestation that he always felt he was still working for Stu. The saddest chapter of the story is, of course, Stewart's early death at age 47: He was in the waiting room of a clinic on December 12, 1985, feeling unwell, when he suffered a heart attack. Four years later, when the Stones were inducted into the Rock and Roll Hall of Fame, the band made certain the citation included Stu's name. They knew, even if many of their fans did not and even if they had denied their cofounder a fair financial shake, that for 23 years there had been six Rolling Stones.

WHO WAS
BRIAN JONES?

IVAN KEEMAN/REDFERNS/GETTY

HE HAD PROBLEMS with so many things—his relationships with women (he could be not only psychologically but physically abusive), his distrust of even his closest friends, his propensity for scheming—but, until substance abuse hindered him, he never had problems with music. He was brilliant on harmonica; and the intricate art of layering rock guitars atop one another, weaving them, reached an early apex in his playing with Richards. Here, Jones soars on sitar during "Paint It Black" on the British telly show *Ready, Steady, Go!* in 1966.

PHILIP TOWNSEND/CAMERA PRESS

Whereas the Beatles were four famous guys and then suddenly the band didn't exist—a nice, linear story—the Rolling Stones, a half century on, have seen various people come and go. We will pause in these pages to focus on some of these folks: the Ians and Brians and Ronnies of the Stones Universe. You have just met Stu, and now here is Brian, who placed the original ad in *Jazz News* summoning interested parties to the Bricklayers Arms pub in London's Soho, where he and Stu would approve of Mick and then also of his friend Keith. What to make of Brian Jones? Whereas everyone liked Ian Stewart, not even Brian's own bandmates enjoyed his company on a regular basis. Brilliant, mercurial, a devoted friend and a mean SOB by turns, talented but insecure about his talents, eventually destabilized by substance abuse: Jones arrived thinking the Stones were his band, and left having been booted out. A different story entirely than Stu's. No less sad.

HE WAS WONDERFUL on guitar in 1963, and his demons had not yet gained the purchase they eventually would. The arrival of Andrew Oldham in this same year would, however, quickly cause problems not just for Ian Stewart but also for Jones. Oldham positioned the Stones brilliantly, but to do so he felt he needed Stewart out, and by necessity he usurped the authority that Jones felt was his. Even as the Stones became famous in England, the problems that would lead to Jones's downfall were begun.

BRIAN WOULD REMAIN a Stone through the decade, but what authority he might once have had was assumed by Andrew Oldham—not to mention by Ian Stewart, innocently with his thorough competency, and by Jagger and Richards, who were writing the songs. Opposite: In 1964, preparing for a performance, attended by a poodle. This page, top: Jones (left), who was a fashion icon in the mid '60s, is seen here with Andy Warhol at a party in New York City in 1966. Above, left: With the Drifters. Above, right: A characteristic pose. Right: In 1965. He would die in '69, found at the bottom of his swimming pool, and while conspiracists will prattle on about murder forever, Brian Jones's end, at age 27, was predictable. He was the first of the so-called 27 Club. Janis, Jimi and Jim joined him—same age when they passed—within two years. Just by the way, Amy Winehouse was 27 when she died in 2011.

"THE ROLLIN' STONES"

BY THE EARLY weeks of 1963 the iteration of the band that would become famous had been set, with, from left, Keith Richards, Brian Jones, and Mick Jagger having been recently joined by Charlie Watts on drums and Bill Wyman on bass. The Stones' manager as they were trying to make their name in the clubs and pubs of London was a Russian named Giorgio Gomelsky, who was tireless in setting up gigs and urging the boys to keep playing: for free at the Ealing Jazz Club, for nickels at the Crawdaddy Club (which was actually just the back room of the Station Hotel's pub in Richmond), for dimes at Ken Colyer's club, Studio 51, in Soho.

JEAN-MARIE PÉRIER/PHOTO 12/POLARIS

As young boys, Mick Jagger and Keith Richards, both born in 1943, had been chums in Dartford, a comfortable commuter town about 15 miles east of London. Then their families moved apart, but one day in 1961 the teens, still students (Richards at Sidcup Art College and Jagger at the London School of Economics) chanced to meet at a train station. Keith noticed that Mick was, like him, carrying records of music he loved: Chuck Berry, Muddy Waters and the like. At the time, blues, R&B and rock 'n' roll bands were being formed on a nightly basis throughout England, and soon Jagger and Richards, along with a third pal, Dick Taylor, formed theirs. Bands were also mutating constantly, and by June of 1962, after the guys auditioned for Ian Stewart and Brian Jones, they found themselves, with drummer Tony Chapman, in a new six-man group. While Jones was on the phone telling *Jazz News* the latest, he was asked what this nascent band was called and glanced at the floor at a Muddy Waters album with a track named "Rollin' Stone." As he spelled it, he too left off the *g*.

JAGGER IS IN full boogie flight and Jones and Richards are weaving their guitar lines— aspects of the Stones that would set them apart—as things are starting to happen for them, and fast. They are not far removed from gigs that played to far fewer fans. Gomelsky remembered a set at the Crawdaddy Club that drew three people (Wyman recalled it as six; both he and Gomelsky noted that the weather had been crummy).

PHOTO 12/POLARIS (3)

KEN COLYER WAS a British jazz trumpeter in the postwar era, and Gomelsky booked his Rollin' Stones into a series of engagements in Colyer's club in London's Soho that began on March 3, 1963. Sometimes, the band would play a set there in the afternoon, hump the gear over to the Crawdaddy Club and play two more 45-minute sets in the evening. They were developing a following, and Gomelsky built the crowd further by offering perks: Bring two friends, get in for free, which certainly appealed to the college kids who were starting to dig the Stones. One day, Gomelsky asked the red-hot Beatles if they wanted to hear his band play. Dressed in matching leather topcoats, John, Paul, George and Ringo caught the second set at the Crawdaddy Club. They loved what they heard, and had a nice inter-band chat afterward. Mick would later recall being in awe of John Lennon, who immediately put him at ease. Mick complimented John on his harmonica playing on the hit "Love Me Do." John demurred that he couldn't play near as well as Mick. It was a veritable musical love fest. The several musicians got on so well, the Beatles invited the Stones to their own show the next week—an invitation that pointed up where each band was at in its career. The Stones, who were still gigging in the clubs, went to see the Beatles' concert at the Royal Albert Hall.

AND SO, the Beatles came to see
the Stones play in Richmond and
the Stones indeed went to see the
Beatles play at the Royal Albert
Hall, where Brian Jones in particular
reacted to the frenzy by repeating,
"This is what we like . . . this is what
we want!" At least some of the blues
purists in the band were now desir-
ous of being pop stars. Their wishes
would be granted almost instantly.
Someone else from the Beatles
camp, a kid who had been working publicity assignments for the
band's manager, Brian Epstein, also
caught the Stones' act: "The day
that Andrew Loog Oldham came to
see us play at Richmond," remembers Keith Richards in his memoir,
"things began to move at devas-
tating speed. Within something
like two weeks we had a recording
contract." And within weeks after
that, Keith (below) and Mick—and
the others—were stars.

PHILIP TOWNSEND/CAMERA PRESS

WE WILL LEARN much more about Andrew Loog Oldham beginning on the very next page, but one more quick note here. To say he was a cheeky teen is to put it mildly. After seeing the Stones in action and being blown away by how energetic and sexy they are, he is on the phone immediately to Brian Jones, who fancies he can make decisions for the group. These machinations are all conducted behind Giorgio Gomelsky's back, of course, and it is Gomelsky's ill fate that he and the Rollin' Stones never signed a management contract. The promises Oldham makes and the quick results he gets mean that the hard-hustling Russian is out and the skinny 19-year-old— "a sharp blade," as Keith calls him in *Life*—is in. When he had worked for Brian Epstein, one of Oldham's principal assignments had been to shape the Beatles' image. As this photograph of the Stones, which was taken in 1963 and looks like it could have been lifted straight out of *A Hard Day's Night*, indicates: At first, Oldham brings to the table what he knows. Soon, however, his ideas expand, and with that so does the Stones' horizon.

WHO IS ANDREW LOOG OLDHAM?

PRECIOUS ABOUT IMAGE, his own as well as his band's, Oldham puts himself in a setting that is just so in October of 1964. The Stones are riding high, and therefore so is Oldham. We have already visited his influence with Stu and Brian. Now we meet him more fully.

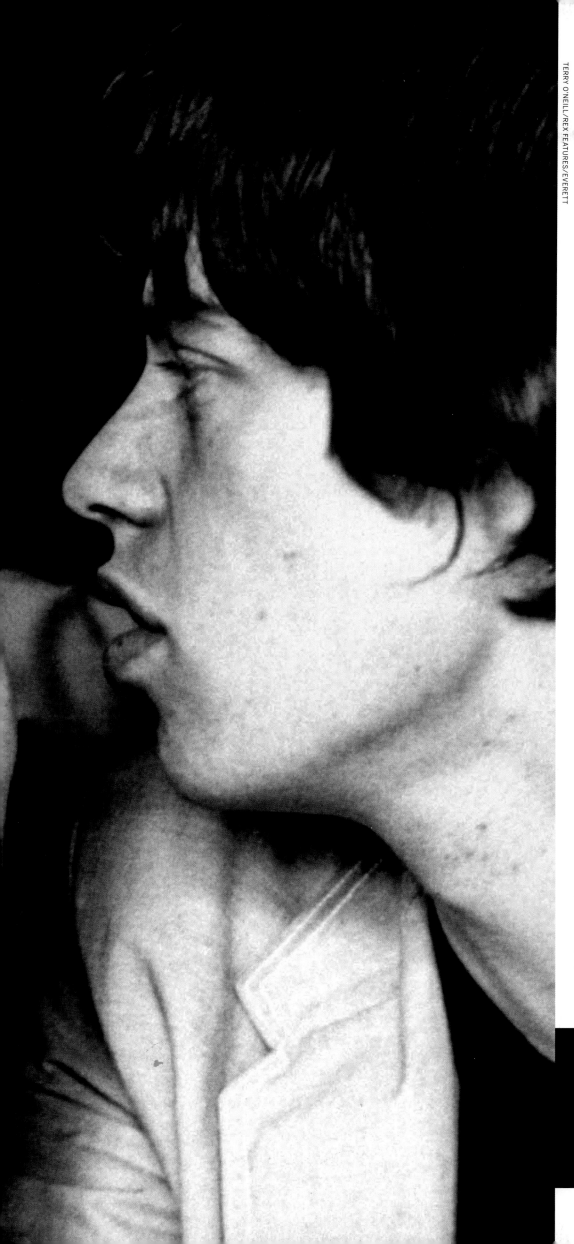

I n a way, the Andrew Oldham story could not be more perfect; it's Carnaby Street Shakespeare. He was an energetic teen associate to Brian Epstein in Epstein's upstart Liverpool management enterprise that all of a sudden had the Beatles, and then he was out on the sidewalk: canned. "I'll show him," the young man said to himself, and before long he found himself a band. He positioned the Stones as the anti-Beatles, which upset John Lennon, since the Beatles actually were the laddies from a hardbitten northern industrial town who had cut their teeth in the strip-circuit clubs of Hamburg, while Mick Jagger was just one of those namby-pamby boys from down south who was adopting some kind of aesthete's appreciation of the blues. But Oldham's strategy was sound, at least at first in England. The audience wanted the bad boys. In America, the relationship was, initially, more complicated, as we shall see. But the Stones had thrown their lot in with Oldham, and he had become their Brian Epstein. Which was exactly what he wanted. Not least, to get back at Brian Epstein.

THE DYNAMIC OF the Stones in 1962 and '63 changed very fast. It was Ian Stewart's band, or Brian Jones's band, but quite quickly it became apparent: It was going nowhere fast unless it was Mick Jagger's band, or unless Mick Jagger was fronting the band. Jagger's approval of Oldham certainly was instrumental in sealing the management deal.

HE WAS VERY much one of the boys—he played on several of the albums, usually incidental contributions—and opposite he is pictured with his friend, the American star Gene Pitney, who has dropped by the studio in 1963 to help with a Stones session. At right, he is seated next to Brian Jones. Oldham was even younger than the band members themselves, and his bravado was something to see. He was flamboyant to a fault, but meantime he produced all Rolling Stones records from 1963 till early 1967—despite having no experience as a producer—and those are pretty great records. He pushed and prodded constantly, and of course that is untenable for a lifelong relationship. He split with the group that latter year, '67, and eventually he relocated to Colombia after marrying an actress and fashion model from that country. He has produced various pop acts there. He is seen below in 2004. Andrew Loog Oldham, who demoted Ian Stewart and busted Brian Jones, was a true piece of work. And he still is.

"WOULD YOU LET YOUR DAUGHTER MARRY A ROLLING STONE?"

"THE WHOLE IDEA of the Beatles and the uniforms, keeping everything uniform, still made sense to Andrew," writes Keith Richards in *Life*. "To us it didn't. He put us in uniforms. We had those damn houndstooth, dogtooth check jackets on *Thank Your Lucky Stars*." Yes, but, while the Beatles were all smokers, they at least tossed the fags when the shutter was about to click. Bill and Mick couldn't be bothered, which was the Rolling Stones' way.

The memorable line that Andrew Oldham poured into the ear of an eager rock journalist not long after Oldham began managing the band was actually: "Would you let your daughter go with a Rolling Stone?" Fleet Street, as was its wont, quickly pumped up the volume to "marry." Oldham didn't mind a bit. His plan was to exaggerate any dark aspects of the band (to whose name he soon added the *g* in "Rolling"). To set the record straight, Oldham did not invent their bad boy image; in fact, he tried to dress the band in matching suits for a short while, à la the Beatles, but the guys quietly rebelled, drifting back to clothes they were comfortable in onstage. This set them apart, as did the rougher, blues-drenched music they were making. According to Wyman, this image developed "completely accidentally. Andrew never did engineer it. He simply exploited it exhaustively." He sure did. The first album in Britain showed five sullen, unsmiling guys on the cover. Ian was kicked offstage in part because he didn't look right. When the Stones got into trouble in a restaurant, Oldham made sure all knew it. He saw something big starting to happen with his "anti-Beatles." In England, suddenly: Stonesmania.

ONCE OLDHAM had become convinced that against-the-grain was the way to go, he encouraged his golden boys to plunge—all in. He saw how the fans were reacting to Mick's (shall we say) gesticulating, and encouraged his frontman to turn it up to 11. Even on television shows, the rude boy's increasingly famous tongue was not put on a leash.

PETER FRANCIS/REDFERNS/GETTY

MIRRORPIX/EVERETT

MONITOR/RETNA/PHOTOSHOT/EVERETT

TERRY O'NEILL/GETTY

THE STONES had caught on in England, certainly, but it took them a short while to become dependable hitmakers there. They had a dynamic live act (top), yet the records they released as singles were all, for a time, covers: Chuck Berry's "Come On," Buddy Holly's "Not Fade Away" and the like. The most interesting in this batch of early Top-40-but-not-Number-One British hits was their second single, Lennon and McCartney's "I Wanna Be Your Man," which would reach Number 12 on the U.K. charts. Let's go back to September 1963: The Stones are in the studio, and they are frustrated that nothing they're playing sounds hit-worthy. Keith picks up the tale: "Andrew had disappeared to walk about and absent himself from this gloom, and he'd walked into John and Paul, getting out of a taxi in the Charing Cross Road. They had a drink and detected Andrew's distress. He told them: no songs. They came back to the studio with him and gave us a song that was on their next album but wasn't coming out as a single, 'I Wanna Be Your Man.' They played it through with us. Brian put on some nice slide guitar; we turned it into an unmistakably Stones rather than a Beatles song. It was clear that we had a hit almost before they left the studio." Oldham realized the Stones desperately needed their own version of Lennon/McCartney. He urged Jagger/Richards (opposite) to take up the challenge. Their first efforts distressed him—"soppy and imitative"—but then the two started to click.

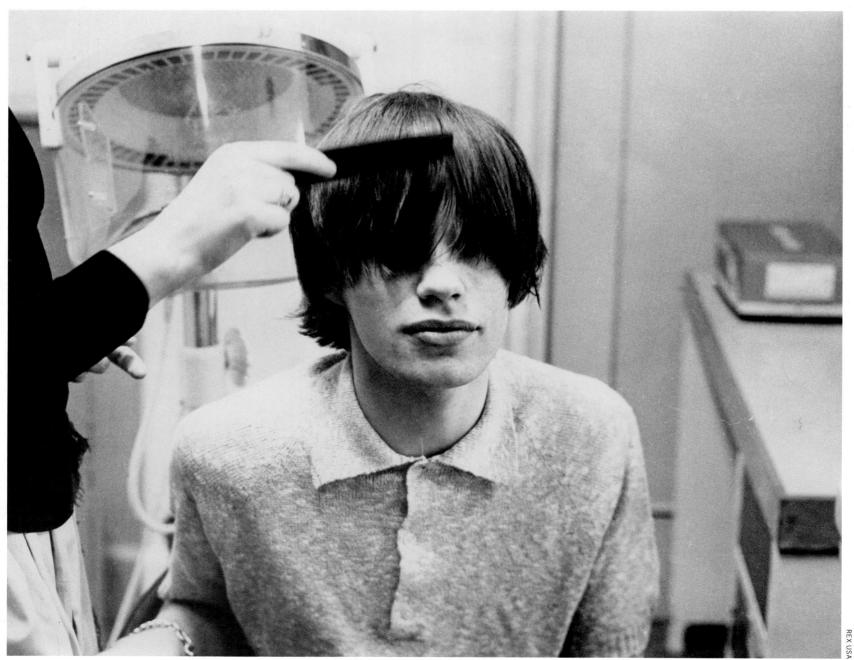

IN THE SWINGIN' LONDON of the early and mid 1960s, music was all, and fashion was equally all. It was the Beatles and Stones, but it was also Twiggy and Mary Quant and the clothing styles of Carnaby Street. And while Oldham (and the boys themselves) were now keen to be nasty and leathery and rough, it also profited them to be "pretty"—it's why Ian Stewart was given the boot. Good piano player, trusted musically, but as he lamented to Richards upon his sacking: "Don't look the same as you, do I?" The fans expected their Stones to take this seriously, and therefore it wasn't at all surprising for Brian to spend a good bit of time before the mirror (opposite, top left) or for Mick to let a camera be present to record his prettification on May 9, 1964, at the BBC Television Centre.

PHILIP TOWNSEND/CAMERA PRESS

AGIP/RUE DES ARCHIVES/GRANGER

MIRRORPIX/EVERETT (3)

THERE WAS STILL a large argument in England in late 1963 and early 1964 as to who was in second place: the Stones, the Dave Clark Five, the Searchers, Gerry and the Pacemakers, later the Who. *Who?* But mere months were endless to kids in those days, and weeks were long too. Slowly (it seemed then) and incredibly rapidly (it seems historically), the Stones emerged. "Maybe it happened to Frank Sinatra, Elvis Presley," writes Richards in *Life.* "I don't think it had ever reached the extremes it got to around the Beatles and the Stones time, at least in England." Opposite, top: Brian and two who would have then been called, by some, "birds." Bottom: Alice, 18, claims to be one of the band's biggest fans. This page, top two photos: Priming the pump of Stonesmania. Above: The mania itself, enacted, on August 13, 1964, at the Palace Ballroom in Douglas on the Isle of Man.

BEING A TEEN idol is exhausting, as Keith, in 1964 London, well illustrates. There are the gigs to play and records to record, and, suddenly, the songs to write with Mick. And then all these young women! "One minute, no chick in the world. No [expletive] way, and they're going la la la la la," Keith writes. "And the next they're sniffing around. And you're going, wow, when I changed from Old Spice to Habit Rouge, things definitely got better. So what is it they want? Fame? The money? Or is it for real? And of course when you've not had much chance with beautiful women, you start to get suspicious." Several of the Stones did not get so philosophical about the situation. (Charlie Watts, who today is approaching his 50th wedding anniversary, was and has been legendarily different, shunning all groupies; once when his bandmates were "hosted" by Hugh Hefner at the Playboy Mansion, he spent the evening down the street at the home of his friend Marshall Chess.) Keith, for his part, and despite being "suspicious" about the women's motives, admits that he dove right in, and told an interviewer that one of his chief laments about the failure of the first U.S. tour (of which we will learn on the next page) was that he couldn't get no action, no satisfaction.

THE STONES DO NOT CONQUER AMERICA

MICK IS CAUGHT in the crush that has become commonplace in England as the Stones are at the airport in June 1964, about to fly to America and are undoubtedly anticipating that they'll duplicate the Beatles' glorious triumph. Disappointment awaits. "The Rolling Stones, when they started, the limits of their ambition was just to be the best [expletive] band in London," Keith writes in his autobiography. "But once the world beckoned, it didn't take long for the scales to fall from the eyes. Suddenly the whole world was opening up, the Beatles were proving that." Ahh, Keith old boy: It ain't that easy, and, just yet, you ain't the Beatles.

BETTMANN/CORBIS

Bill Wyman later termed it "a disaster." The "it" was the band's first U.S. tour: a dozen dates in June of 1964. The British Invasion had famously been launched that February when the Beatles played *The Ed Sullivan Show,* then traveled to Washington, D.C., and, with "I Want to Hold Your Hand" at Number One, played to an audience crazed with delight. As Wyman recalled, "When we arrived, we didn't have a hit record [there] or anything going for us." Keith Richards remembered playing to 600 people in a hall that seated 15,000; and the whole enterprise concluded with the Stones being dissed on *The Hollywood Palace* TV show by host Dean Martin: "Now something for the youngsters," he slurred, "five singin' boys from England . . . Don't know what they're singing about, but here they are." Richards said later: "If Dean Martin listened to us a little more he wouldn't have been quite so flippant. At that time it was a deadly insult, but all it did, all those things, they only went to make us prove ourselves more so we'd come back and bite your head off."

WHEN THE BEATLES had arrived earlier in the year at JFK International Airport, the fans were there screaming, tearing their hair, rending their garments, and a throng of press was present to record every utterance and take every picture from every angle. Not so this time, but that was probably just as well. The Stones, who can be glib and charming, were now in full anti-Beatle mode (at least publicly, as they crafted their image) and might have been off-putting had they been granted a larger platform. But that had not happened, and so what can we say about this sedate June 1, 1964, photograph of their arrival in the States? At least there were flowers—and a day-early birthday cake for Charlie.

NO NEED to keep the fans at bay. At top: The boys pose for the obligatory photo—it's like paying obeisance—with influential New York City DJ Murray the K, who is still promoting himself as being the Fifth Beatle but is uneager to make any claims as the Sixth Stone. Above: Charlie and Keith on the beach in Malibu in June 1964. "There was the stark thing you discovered about America," Keith writes later. "It was civilized round the edges, but fifty miles inland from any major American city, whether it was New York, Chicago, LA or Washington, you really did go into another world." Which is his way of saying: They didn't know who in the world we were. Or as Keith might *actually* put it: They didn't know who in the [expletive] world we [expletive] were. Right: Keith and Andrew, no cordon of security necessary, are ready to head home.

SECOND TIME'S A CHARM

THEY HAD NOT received a hero's welcome necessarily, but immediately upon returning to England, the Stones regain their momentum (here, they perform on the British TV show *Thank Your Lucky Stars* on June 6, 1965, with Brian, Mick and Keith really laying into it). Also, crucially, Jagger and Richards are beginning to find their stride as songwriters (which will further alienate Jones from his cofounding partners). Stones singles begin to become hits on both sides of the pond.

Some good came out of the Stones' first shot at America. Keith Richards later recalled that with everything easy in England, adulation and young women available on a nightly basis, a sterner test was useful. When playing to nobody (and no women) in Omaha, "we really had to work hard . . . and it really got the band together." The band was very together by later in '64 when it recorded a performance for *The TAMI Show,* a feature film that was to counterpoise American rock stars and British Invasion acts. The Stones segment was so good, it wound up following James Brown's act, and Mick later recalled that the soul star was none too pleased. At Andrew Oldham's urging, Mick and Keith continued their apprenticeship in songwriting, and soon the original hits started to flow. At the tail end of 1964 came the first single with Stones originals on both sides: "Heart of Stone" backed with "What a Shame." It reached Number 19 on the U.S. charts. As the Ramones much later articulated: *"Hey ho, let's go!"*

THAT'S BETTER: a proper, Beatlesque arrival-in-America picture. They have now enjoyed Number One hits in England—the first being their cover of Bobby and Shirley Womack's "It's All Over Now," recorded during the earlier U.S. trip at Chess Records in Chicago, where they'd met Muddy Waters— and finally America is ready to meet the Rolling Stones.

EVERETT (2)

THE EXCITEMENT, ENTERTAINMENT AND MUSIC OF TEENAGE AMERICA!

Starring

THE **BEACH BOYS**
CHUCK BERRY
JAMES BROWN
AND THE **FLAMES**
THE **BARBARIANS**
MARVIN GAYE
GERRY AND THE
PACEMAKERS
LESLEY GORE
JAN AND **DEAN**
BILLY J. KRAMER
AND THE **DAKOTAS**
SMOKEY ROBINSON
AND THE **MIRACLES**
THE **SUPREMES**
THE **ROLLING
STONES** IN

THE FIRST ANNUAL

T·A·M·I SHOW

TEENAGE AWARDS MUSIC INTERNATIONAL

ELECTRONOVISION
A PRODUCT OF SCREEN ENTERTAINMENT CO.

EVEN BEFORE they enjoy their first U.S. hit in July 1965, they are seen on American screens in dynamic performances that have none of the awkwardness—or impolite dismissiveness—of that Dean Martin show. In fact, on the multi-act *TAMI Show,* the Stones, whose performance is riveting, are chosen as the closing act, which is taken as an insult by no less than the hardest-working man in show business. "We weren't actually following James Brown because there were hours in between the filming of each section," Mick remembered later. "Nevertheless, he was still very annoyed about it." Annoyed, too, is Ed Sullivan, on whose show the band debuts on October 25, 1964. The crowd goes so crazy— more than Beatles crazy—that the host bans the band forevermore. "Forevermore" proves mutable—in fact, it proves a very short time— because the Stones can no longer be denied, and they, like the Beatles, will appear on *Sullivan* regularly in the next few years (right, their fourth appearance, September 11, 1966).

JEAN-MARIE PÉRIER/PHOTO 12/POLARIS

TERRY O'NEILL/GETTY

OPPOSITE: Keith tunes up in Los Angeles. On this page, scenes from TV shows filmed in London (the Stones appeared on the popular *Ready, Steady, Go!* 26 times from 1963 through 1966). In this period, the Stones are solidifying their status as England's number two band and as challengers to the lovable moptops in America, and are also beginning to indicate that they may have a future longer and brighter than most. They have released, in February 1965, the Jagger/Richards song "The Last Time," which is their first original composition to reach the top of the U.K. singles chart, meanwhile going Top 10 in the U.S. "It gave us a level of confidence; a pathway of how to do it," Keith later says. This song was the "bridge into thinking about writing for the Stones."

MICHAEL OCHS ARCHIVES/GETTY

PETER FRANCIS/REDFERNS/GETTY

THE BEATLES AND THE STONES

HIS EXPRESSION indicates that Charlie Watts is being read the latest pop news by Mick Jagger, and that he is fully cognizant that the Fab Four are still (and probably forever will be) in first place— they've gotten their MBEs for goodness' sake. But in fact the inter-band rivalry is more than friendly. It is positively chummy.

A great secret of the '60s, vigorously concealed by Andrew Oldham, was: The guys in these two groups really liked the other guys. Mick and Keith were in awe of John's and Paul's songwriting prowess, and they were blown away by the Beatles' generosity in handing over "I Wanna Be Your Man." John in particular coveted the Stones' bad boy image, and chose to hang out when he might (his LSD road trip with Keith, as recounted in *Life,* is a trip worth revisiting). Even as Oldham forwarded his anti-Beatles campaign, the Beatles and the Stones grew closer. It must have driven Oldham crazy to see Mick chanting along during the filming of the performance of "All You Need Is Love," which would be seen worldwide by 350 million via satellite TV in 1967. His frontman looked like a flower-power wimp. But . . . Maybe it didn't drive him crazy at all. He surely realized by then that the Beatles would always be bigger, and that sidling up to the Fab Four might be good for his Stones. Regardless, there was nothing he could do about it. Many of these nine musicians weren't just friendly rivals, they were, by now, mates.

IN 1964, the big story is the Beatles, who are conquering the world this year while the Stones are failing miserably in their own first attempt, and here we have a hilarious expression of the pecking order: a tuxedoed Paul McCartney greeting his friends Keith Richards and Brian Jones after they have crashed a fancy-pants party for the Beatles.

OPPOSITE: Mick, left, is just as groovy as John Lennon in 1967 after the Beatles have led their generation—and the Stones—into psychedelia (which results in, for the Stones, the unfortunate album *Their Satanic Majesties Request*). Above, clockwise from top left: Mick (right) hobnobs with George Harrison (left) and Lennon (center) at the height of the earlier, "fab" days; Mick and John exchange greetings on December 11, 1968, at the taping of "The Rolling Stones Rock and Roll Circus"; and then, during that show, John performs in public without the Beatles for the first time, leading a supergroup called the Dirty Mac that includes, from left, lead guitarist Eric Clapton, drummer Mitch Mitchell (of the Jimi Hendrix Experience) and, in this instance, bass guitarist Keith Richards.

THE YEAR IS 1966, Paul McCartney and Mick Jagger are just about the biggest things in the world. Paul is in the studio helping Mick's girlfriend and his own good friend, Marianne Faithfull (middle photo in the sequence opposite), with some backing vocals. "We were always friendly," Jagger later remembered of the Beatles, who had been kind enough to show up—let's say, to grace—an early Stones gig when they were still playing rhythm and blues in the pubs. "But after the Beatles and the Stones stopped playing clubs, we didn't see each other that much. We were on tour or they were on tour. And in a way we were in competition in those days. Brian Jones, more than any of us, felt we were in competition . . . But we were friendly with them, I must say." In this case, Mick, Paul and Marianne were all in London at the same time, so why not get together?

THEY STILL GET together, those who are left. Ronnie Wood jammed with Paul McCartney in 2011 in London during Sir Paul's triumphant concert there, because they are British rock royalty and that's the way it is. Here, in 1978, Paul's wife and bandmate, Linda, indulges the two as they have a laugh at a session. In Keith Richards's autobiography, *Life,* there are marvelous passages about the survivors of the '60s scene, none of these episodes more moving than the ones about Sir Paul making his way unannounced to Keith's place while Paul's marriage to Heather Mills is expiring. No reason, just to talk about what used to be. Because there was no one else who could understand

SATISFACTION, AND NOT

THANK GOODNESS they had Charlie. The estimable Mr. Watts, gentleman percussionist, was given to the finer things in life, and in matters sartorial leaned toward splendor, amassing, once the hits climbed the charts and the money started to pour in, a considerable collection of bespoke suits. He knew Savile Row like other Londoners of his age knew Carnaby Street. Certainly at the time, Mick, Brian and Keith chuckled about this. But photographs live on, and who's laughing now?

JOHN READER/GETTY

One night Keith Richards awoke with "(I Can't Get No) Satisfaction" in his head—the riff, the melody, the whole thing, minus words. This would be the band's first Number One international hit, and "Get Off of My Cloud" would be their second. The Stones were as big as big could be (this side of the Beatles), and their initial faux cockiness was turning into the real thing. The four of them (excepting the always properly mannered Charlie Watts) strutted like Mick, morning, noon and night. They got wasted on booze, took lots of drugs, got busted—it was all part of being a Rolling Stone. And all the while, they made better and better records: also part of being a Rolling Stone. Individually, they started to fall apart: This, too, would be part of being a Rolling Stone, although it wasn't yet foreseen. Finally, one of the original guys—Brian—got fired, and then he died. The Stones memorialized him properly. Not long thereafter, all hell broke loose at a concert in California, and someone else died. The band and its ex-manager Oldham had always promoted the dark side of the Stones. That was no longer necessary.

THE GLIMMER TWINS are not yet born, but they are conceived. With Andrew Oldham's encouragement—at his urging—Mick and Keith essentially take over the band. Initially, there are some group compositions credited to Nanker/ Phelge, a nonexistent team of composers. But it eventuates that Brian can't write songs, Charlie's and Bill's contributions are minimal, and the product comes from Jagger/Richards.

IN THE 1960S, the Stones never took the wages of sin too very seriously. Opposite: Did Brian Jones intend to impress the judge with his sensationally striped suit when answering drug charges in London on June 2, 1967? That same year, Keith and Mick are hauled in during the notorious Redlands bust at Keith's place in Sussex. One of the Beatles had also been there during the weekend-long shebang, but the coppers weren't interested in goody-two-shoes Beatles, they were after the insolent Stones. Jagger's girlfriend Marianne Faithfull was named in filings for the Redlands raid as Miss X, and it was alleged that Miss X was wearing nothing but a fur rug when the law arrived—a rug she deliberately "let fall" during proceedings. Jagger and Richards were convicted on drug charges and sentenced to prison for three months and 12 months, respectively. On appeal to Britain's Lord Chief Justice, Richards's conviction was overturned and Jagger's sentence was reduced to probation. Right: Two years later, Faithfull, fully frocked, stands faithfully by her man after the two have answered marijuana-possession charges in Marlborough Street Magistrates Court (below, the mug shots in this case). Mick eventually pays the equivalent of a $390 fine. Of course, drugs will rear their ugly head time and again as the Stones saga spools forward. Keith's heroin use is one of the most famous celebrity-addiction stories of all time. As for the legendary chapter in which he gets a full-body blood transfusion in order to wean him off the drug: Keith mentions it in his autobiography, then says that he will never confirm or deny.

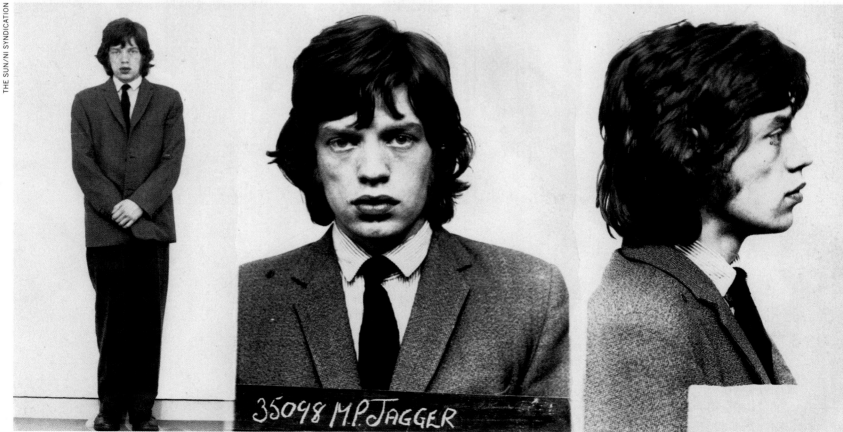

35098 M.P. JAGGER

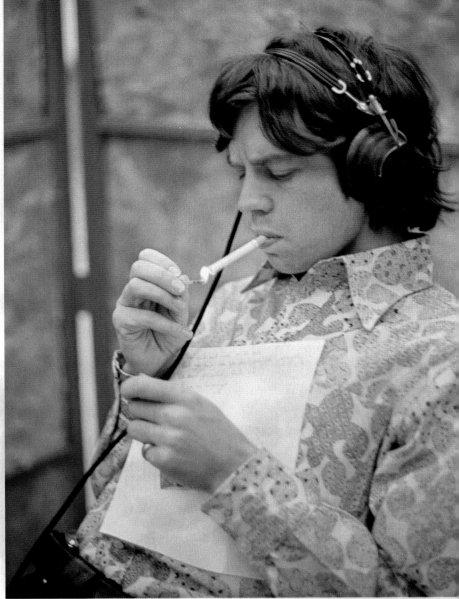

OPPOSITE, clockwise from top: Keith strums in 1964; Charlie bites his nails; Keith, Andrew, Charlie and Stu monitor a recording. Andrew Oldham was more musical than Brian Epstein, surely—he sat in on many a session, often on some kind of percussion, and was credited as producer on seminal recordings and as a co-writer of "As Tears Go By." Keith imagined horns on "Satisfaction," but Andrew put it out as it existed, unbeknownst to the band—a smart move, as history has proved. But Andrew's true talents and largest contributions were in schmoozing and arm-twisting. As for Stu, even as the others began to ascend, his continuing influence was great, and is captured by Keith, in *Life,* in a brief anecdote about "The Last Time": "That was when it really clicked, with that song, when Mick and I felt confident enough to actually lay it in front of Brian and Charlie and Ian Stewart, arbiter of events. With those earlier songs we would have been chased out of the room. But that song defined us in a way, and went to number one in the UK." This page, clockwise from top left: Keith is doing the rock thing, wearing sunglasses indoors; Mick lights up; Mick sings while Keith pays attention.

OPPOSITE, clockwise from top: Keith, very self-satisfied, with his favorite-ever car, Blue Lena (named for Lena Horne), his Bentley Continental Flying Spur (which during a drive in Morocco in search of drugs led to him and Anita Pallenberg falling in, ahem, love); sliding down a bannister in August 1965 in Paris; at his beloved country home in Sussex, Redlands (where he and Mick would be caught in a drug raid in 1967, as we will shortly learn). This page, above, Mick and Keith and vices: Smoking and drinking in '67, though we don't see the habit that will get them and also Brian busted this year—drug-taking. Below: The band, wholesomely, in a diner. Ingesting food. Drinking milk.

IN THE 1960S, the Stones never took the wages of sin too very seriously. Opposite: Did Brian Jones intend to impress the judge with his sensationally striped suit when answering drug charges in London on June 2, 1967? That same year, Keith and Mick are hauled in during the notorious Redlands bust at Keith's place in Sussex. One of the Beatles had also been there during the weekend-long shebang, but the coppers weren't interested in goody-two-shoes Beatles, they were after the insolent Stones. Jagger's girlfriend Marianne Faithfull was named in filings for the Redlands raid as Miss X, and it was alleged that Miss X was wearing nothing but a fur rug when the law arrived—a rug she deliberately "let fall" during proceedings. Jagger and Richards were convicted on drug charges and sentenced to prison for three months and 12 months, respectively. On appeal to Britain's Lord Chief Justice, Richards's conviction was overturned and Jagger's sentence was reduced to probation. Right: Two years later, Faithfull, fully frocked, stands faithfully by her man after the two have answered marijuana-possession charges in Marlborough Street Magistrates Court (below, the mug shots in this case). Mick eventually pays the equivalent of a $390 fine. Of course, drugs will rear their ugly head time and again as the Stones saga spools forward. Keith's heroin use is one of the most famous celebrity-addiction stories of all time. As for the legendary chapter in which he gets a full-body blood transfusion in order to wean him off the drug: Keith mentions it in his autobiography, then says that he will never confirm or deny.

35098 M.P. JAGGER

MICK AND KEITH are now two of the world's biggest rock stars, and befitting that status they disport with two of youthdom's most phenomenal girlfriends (and, as rock stars seemingly must, they cheat on each other by bedding the other's paramour, according to Keith's book). Opposite, clockwise from top left, Keith and Italian-born actress Anita Pallenberg in three photographs: In Cannes in 1967; chilling at home in London in 1969; and with their baby son, Marlon, in August of that same year. Below, clockwise from top left: Mick and Marianne in March 1967; an affectionate moment; and with Marianne's son, Nicholas, from her earlier marriage (she left her husband for Jagger). Faithfull, whose recording career was launched when Andrew Oldham, having met her at a party, gave her the song "As Tears Go By," became best friends with Pallenberg. She developed a horrible drug addiction in the 1960s and co-wrote "Sister Morphine" for the Stones' *Sticky Fingers* album. A survivor, she continues to record today. Pallenberg, according to Keith, was also a heroin addict, and Mick once said she "nearly killed me" with the drugs she brought into the band. She and Keith stayed together a long time—until 1980—and had two more children together: a daughter, Angela (called by them Dandelion), in 1972, and a second son, Tara, in 1976. That boy died 10 weeks after his birth. Today Pallenberg, also a survivor, spends most of her time in Europe, keeps her hand in acting, and also enjoys growing vegetables and drawing.

EVERETT

CENTRAL PRESS/HULTON/GETTY

BETTMANN/CORBIS

AS THE STONES become more popular and increasingly flaunt their flamboyance—not to mention their dark side—things grow ever crazier, and ever more dangerous. Opposite: Bill, Brian and Keith board a flight from London Airport (now Heathrow) in 1967, heading out for a gig abroad. Above: On April 14 of that year, 12,000 fans riot during a concert in Zurich, Switzerland. What had happened: A frenzied few had rushed the stage, and one of them had fallen, sustaining a fractured skull. Hundreds of others, as if smelling blood, leapt in; 250 policemen and 150 security guards went to work. This was a precursor of events to unfold in 1969. That year, the Stones' crucible begins with the death of the recently fired Brian Jones. Below: Scenes at St. Mary's parish church in Cheltenham, England, on July 10. The wreath is from Mick and Marianne, with a farewell note from Mick.

MIRRORPIX/EVERETT

MICHAEL WEBB/KEYSTONE/GETTY

MICHAEL CHARITY/CAMERA PRESS

ON A FINE DAY in July of 1969, 300,000 fans pour into London's Hyde Park for a free concert by the Stones in tribute to the band's late cofounder, Brian Jones. Things had not ended well between Brian and the others, but you cannot tell this as Mick reads movingly (opposite) and sings fiercely (top), while Keith (with Mick, above right) churns with the band's new guitarist, Mick Taylor, who is making his stage debut with them today. In the immense crowd are Anita Pallenberg (left, with headband) and Marianne Faithfull with her son, Nicholas; regardless of all the anonymous thousands, this is a family affair. Already, rumors are circulating among the crowd that Brian was addled, or that Brian was murdered—that Brian was an enemy-maker who ran up against an enemy he couldn't handle. This last bit is certainly true, whether the enemy was someone else, drugs or life itself. The Stones, clearly, are determined to carry on, as they were only yesterday when they booted Brian and hired Mick Taylor. That they are still with us as a band, more than

ALTAMONT: What a way to end the '60s. (Some do say: What a *fitting* way to end the '60s.) The Stones are now the baddest band on the planet (this is way before the Sex Pistols, and such as Black Sabbath are only forming), and if they have a theme song on this tour, it might as well be "Sympathy for the Devil." They certainly do sense that things are other than they should be on December 6, 1969, at Altamont Speedway in California, where they have agreed to headline and have agreed to allow the Hells Angels to assist in crowd control. (What a great idea.) When things are going relatively well during the set, Mick preens and struts for the audience (opposite) and he and Keith exult (top). Then the crowd's craziness starts to be met by brute force, and Mick, for all his stage skills, cannot control the situation (above, left). A young man named Meredith Hunter is killed right in front of the stage. Woodstock Nation has been stabbed as well, and the idea that rock fests are about peace and community and "free love" is thoroughly cooked. In the final photograph, Mick watches the critical instant in footage from the Maysles Brothers documentary *Gimme Shelter* and remains attentive but dispassionate. He seems to be asking: It wasn't our fault, was it? It couldn't have been our fault, right?

WHO IS MICK TAYLOR?

IF TAYLOR, in the foreground, looks so much younger than Charlie Watts in this 1969 picture, it's because he is at least five years younger than all his bandmates and seven years behind Charlie. But he has arrived nominated by John Mayall, seconded by Keith and with a prodigy's talent. "He seemed just to step in naturally at the time," writes Keith in *Life*. "Everybody was looking at me, because I was the other guitar player, but my position was, I'd play with anybody. We could only find out by playing together. And we did the most brilliant stuff together, some of the most brilliant stuff the Stones ever did."

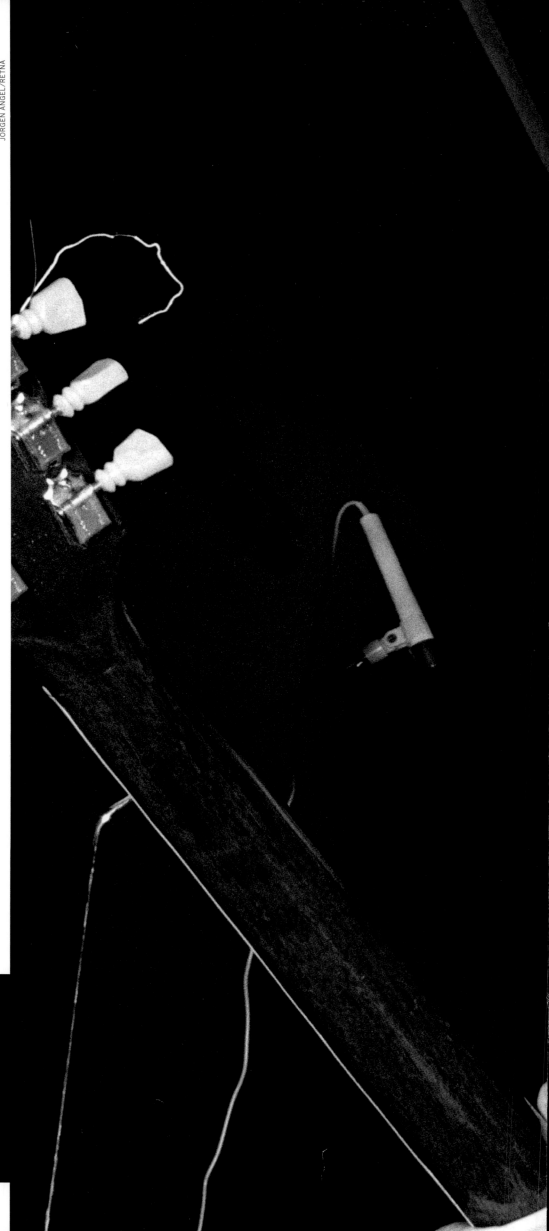

JORGEN ANGEL/RETNA

He had been playing in John Mayall's Bluesbreakers, whence Eric Clapton had sprung, since he was 16. When, in 1969, Mayall heard Brian Jones was being booted from the Stones, he told Mick Jagger that Taylor was the goods. Taylor didn't know what was up; he thought he was being used as a session musician, adding guitar parts on a few songs (including "Honky Tonk Women"). Suddenly, Jones died, the Stones were playing the Hyde Park tribute, Taylor was part of the band. The standard wisdom is that he added a musicality in this middle period, and that is surely true: When Keith was crunching chords early with Brian Jones or later with Ronnie Wood, that was one thing; when he was weaving with Mick Taylor, of whom he was in awe, it was something else. Taylor's playing is all over classic albums like *Sticky Fingers* and *Exile on Main St.,* but he felt he wasn't getting credit for songs he helped invent. He quit the Stones in 1974, astonishing Mick and Keith and millions of fans. Jagger later told *Rolling Stone* of the Mick Taylor period: "Some people think that's the best version of the band that existed."

RIGHT: Mick Taylor, afire with the Stones, in 1968. "Everything was there in his playing—the melodic touch, a beautiful sustain and a way of reading a song," writes Keith. "He had a lovely sound, some very soulful stuff. He'd get where I was going even before I did. I was in awe sometimes listening to Mick Taylor, especially on that slide—try it on 'Love in Vain.' Sometimes just jamming, warming up with him, I'd go, whoa. I guess that's where the emotion came out. I loved the guy, I loved to work with him, but he was very shy and very distant."

LET IT BLEED

IT HAS OFTEN been said of the surviving Stones that they have defied the passage of time; and when you take into account their often hazardous lifestyles, they have seemed to spit in time's eye. Consider once more the photograph on pages eight and nine of our book: The band is still finding its feisty nature in Hamburg, Germany, in 1965. Here, back in that country—in Frankfurt—11 years later, the Stones are at the height of their powers, and Mick is fit and flying: He is in his prime. Ten years, 20 years, 30 years on, he would still be bringing it.

The twin blows of Brian Jones's death and the killing of young Meredith Hunter certainly stunned the Stones, but it didn't slow them down. "Mick Taylor being in the band on that '69 tour certainly sealed the Stones together again," writes Keith in *Life,* and there were other key collaborators as well: the producer Jimmy Miller, the pianist Nicky Hopkins, the horn players Bobby Keys and Jim Price. *Sticky Fingers* was made largely in England, then the band relocated to France for tax reasons in 1971 and cut *Exile on Main St.*—considered by many to be the Stones' finest hour. That it got made at all seems, these years later, something of a miracle, as drugs—hard drugs—were now a big part of the Stones' scene. "Maybe I would crash out, if I crashed out at all, around ten in the morning," writes Keith, "get up around four in the afternoon, subject to the usual variations . . . I suppose the schedule was rather strange. It became known as Keith Time, which in Bill Wyman's case made him a little cranky." Eventually Richards went cold turkey on his heroin addiction at a clinic in Switzerland, the record came out and the Stones soldiered on. They started touring in their own airplane with the huge tongue painted on the side, and their entourage—groupies and drug dealers included—grew larger by the week. The band had become an enterprise—and, also, a circus.

BRINGING IT ALL back home: The death of one of the Stones' cofounders certainly caused some introspection among the survivors, and here the band returns to its roots and plays a date at the Marquee Club on Wardour Street in London, the very first place Mick and Keith and four others appeared as the Rollin' Stones in 1962. Between them is the new kid, Mick Taylor.

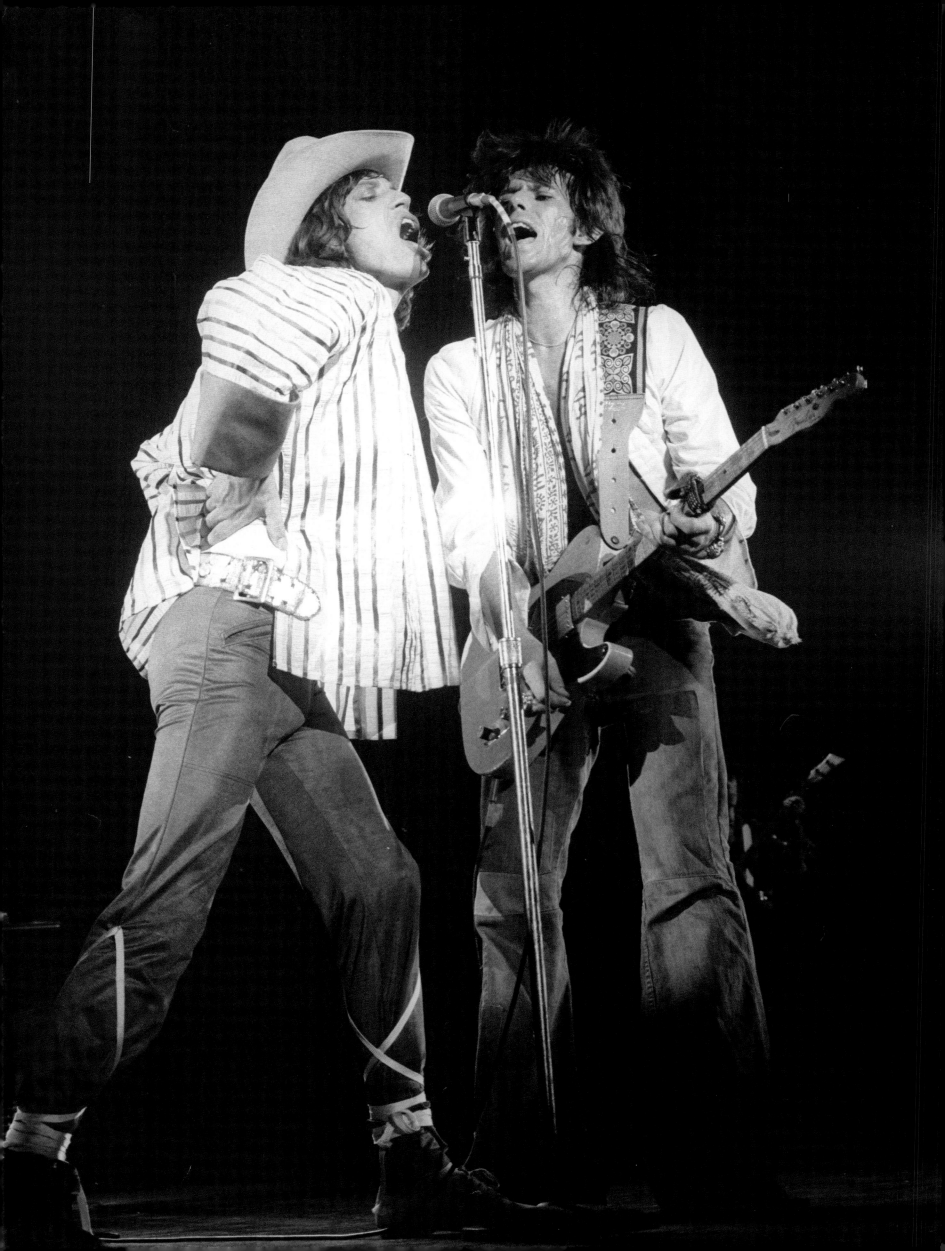

IT WAS THEIR BAND NOW, no question about it. Andrew Oldham, who developed his own massive drug problem, had left during the addled sessions for *Their Satanic Majesties Request* back in 1967. Brian was now dead. Mick and Keith were writing all the songs and making all the decisions. Back in the winter of 1968–69, the two mates and their girlfriends had been on a cruise ship and an elderly English couple asked these exotics who they were: "Just give us a glimmer?" Mick and Keith took to calling themselves the Glimmer Twins, and now, beginning with *It's Only Rock 'n' Roll* in 1974, these Glimmer Twins, not "The Rolling Stones," were listed as producers of the band's albums (sometimes in collaboration with others, such as Don Was). The Stones' sound evolved subtly, and often wonderfully, in this time. Mick and Keith had certainly been influenced by country music earlier—"Sittin' on a Fence" was written in 1965—but "Honky Tonk Women" (and its earlier acoustic version on the *Let It Bleed* album, "Country Honk") became one of their all-time signature songs and went to Number One on both sides of the Atlantic. Onstage, the Stones adopted personas, acted out and started their march toward spectacle (opposite); offstage, they weren't kids anymore (above).

AS JUST SAID: "Offstage, they weren't kids anymore." Mick, Keith and the others were accruing adult responsibilities—it's what life does to a person. Included in these was family. Opposite: Mick met the Nicaragua-born actress and model Bianca Pérez-Mora Macias during an after-concert party in France in 1970, and they wed in a Roman Catholic ceremony on May 12 of the following year, when Bianca was four months pregnant with their daughter, whom they would name Jade. (That baby, bottom, now grown, has made Mick and Bianca twice grandparents.) The Jaggers' union would last until 1978, and after divorcing Mick, Bianca would gradually morph from nightclub habitué to globe-trotting humanitarian, contributing to every cause: women's rights, children's rights, you name it. Meantime, Keith and Anita (top) had a second child, Angela, in 1972, though they would never marry; their oldest, Marlon, is seen in both photos (the one with Mick was taken at Wembley Stadium during the Stones' 1973 European tour). Above, right, is Charlie Watts

WHO IS RONNIE WOOD?

THE OTHERS WHO played with them and have come and gone—Ian Stewart and Brian Jones, who have shuffled off this mortal coil, and Bill Wyman and Mick Taylor—will always be associated, first, with the Rolling Stones. In the case of Ronnie Wood, who has now been with them forever, that is not so clear. He has proved a great partner for Keith onstage, and Keith knew this would be so from the first, heard it when he was freelancing on Wood's solo album in 1973: "Ronnie and I hit it off straightaway, day in, day out, we had a load of good laughs." Laughs: as Ronnie already had had with his mates in the Faces (seen here with lead singer Rod Stewart in the mid 1970s). He played on all of the Faces' hits and was responsible for many of them; it was his band as much as anyone's. Most of the Stones' hits had charted before Wood's time in the group, and though he and Keith have enlivened them night after night ever since, that's not the same. Ronnie Wood has been more than a hired gun, certainly; he's Ronnie Wood, after all. But how much more?

When Mick Taylor rather abruptly left the Stones, the question immediately became: Who next? This had never been a one-guitar band, as good as Keith was. It was always about the interplay, a thing Keith believed in deeply. Ronnie Wood was certainly a candidate out there in the rockosphere. He was a good friend of Keith's and played not unlike him (he said he had been inspired to master slide guitar after hearing Duane Allman back Aretha Franklin, which is just the kind of thing Keith might have said, were he a few years younger). He had asked Keith and Mick to play on his first solo album in 1973, even as he continued with his band, the Faces, fronted by Rod Stewart. It was Keith who asked Ronnie to join the Stones, which Ronnie did way back in 1975. Ronnie has been the second guitarist ever since—more than three times the combined tenure of Brian Jones and Mick Taylor. He has done the Stones thing (addiction, rehab, etc.) many times, and then has set himself up for the next tour. That's what it was to be a Face, and that's what it has been to be a Stone.

AS WITH KEITH, rock 'n' roll was, for Ronnie, an interruption from art school. But in his case, it wasn't a complete interruption. He kept at his painting through the years, and once he was at the center of the world in which he would forever live, pop culture became his great topic. (If you don't know the subject of the painting at left, you don't know Jack.) Ronnie has received acclaim for his work, and has had one-man exhibitions staged in his honor. Musicians are artistic people by nature, and several of them—Joni Mitchell, Tony Bennett, Bob Dylan—have done more than dabble with their painting. Ronnie Wood has done more than dabble.

HARRY BORDEN/OUTLINE/CORBIS

STONES
ALONE

THE BAND'S various freelance projects have been seen by millions, but certainly no other has been witnessed by so many as has Keith's turn as Captain Teague in *Pirates of the Caribbean: At World's End.* (He reprised the role in the fourth *Pirates* film, *On Stranger Tides.*) Richards recalls *Pirates* in his memoirs as "a project that started off with [Johnny] Depp asking me if I minded his using me as a model for his original performance. All I taught him was how to walk around a corner when you're drunk—never moving your back away from the wall. The rest was his." He adds of his own experience on the set: "I had a great time. I got famous for being two-take Richards."

ROBERT MATHEU/RETNA

EVERETT

HENRY DILTZ/CORBIS

GRAHAM WILTSHIRE/REDFERNS/GETTY

One way to keep life fresh is to keep it varied. The Stones determined early that they needed vacations from recording, from touring, from one another. They spread their wings musically. Keith formed a side band, the X-Pensive Winos and, as one of the world's pre-eminent rock guitarists, backed singers such as Lennon and Dylan. Mick pursued a solo career, sang dozens of duets (notably, with Tina Turner) and recently collaborated in the supergroup SuperHeavy. Charlie indulged his love of jazz by forming various ensembles. Ronnie has regularly revisited his old Faces mate Rod Stewart and co-fronted the New Barbarians along with Keith. Ronnie, as mentioned earlier, is also an accomplished painter, continuing a pursuit nourished long ago in art school. He and Keith are authors, too, with Keith's *Life,* oft-cited in these pages, being an acclaimed and best-selling memoir in 2010. Mick had an acting career, and Keith has been both an actor and an actor's muse in those *Pirates of the Caribbean* movies: art imitating life, and then vice versa.

TIME OFF from the day job. Opposite: Mick and Tina get down and dirty at the Live Aid concert in Philadelphia in 1985. This page, from top: Mick in a starring screen role, in Donald Cammell's *Performance,* in 1970; Ronnie and Keith sharing lead vocals with the New Barbarians in 1979; Charlie driving the boogie-woogie band Rocket 88, in which he and Ian Stewart played in the late '70s and early '80s. Of the most well-remembered after-hours bands, Keith was in both (or all three, if you count John Lennon's Dirty Mac), but the Barbarians were actually Ronnie's deal. "I was basically just a side-man, hired for the tour," Keith writes in *Life.* "I can't even remember much of it, it was so much fun." He had said such a thing before, and may yet again.

"THE GREATEST ROCK AND ROLL BAND IN THE WORLD"

THE STONES were happy to make that claim and backed it up with tour after successful tour—breaking records each time out, and only occasionally letting an audience down. (We'll read of a rare instance of that on the following pages.) In this happy portrait made in 1986, we still have four from the 1962 lineup (from left, Bill, Charlie, Keith and Mick), now joined by the heir to Brian Jones and Mick Taylor: Ronnie Wood. Bill would resign in 1992, and has since written books, opened a bistro called the Sticky Fingers Café and started his own, smaller-scale band, Bill Wyman's Rhythm Kings. His primary replacement on bass guitar since 1993, the American Darryl Jones, is a salaried employee of the Stones and has never formally joined the band—which is now, technically and for financial reasons, a quartet.

The Rolling Stones haven't made an impact with new material for a while; it seems the best Jagger/Richards songs have all been written. Nevertheless, the Stones have honed their live performance to perfection, and when they take their show on the road, they pack the largest stadiums, and few leave disappointed. Yes, there are the occasions, as in Finland not too long ago, when one or another Stone—in that case, Keith—takes the stage worse for wear. "He fell on his ass several times during the show in front of 45,000 fans," complained a concert-goer on the fansite It's Only Rock'n Roll. "Some fans claim it's cool, but I'm afraid that Keith believes in his myth too much. I love Keith but it's becoming a little too embarrassing." Keith rebounded, of course; he is a master of rebound. And Mick: He is more of a marvel than ever. A fitness freak, he still sprints the stage as he approaches age 70. Fifty years after passing their audition with Stu and Brian, the two original Stones, plus Charlie, roll on. The members of this band are not indestructible—history has proved that. But, in our time, the band itself seems to be so.

MICK HAS NOT taken a tumble here in Houston in 1978. He, after all, would not be the likely one to take a tumble; that might be Keith or Ronnie (who himself will check into rehab no fewer than eight times through the years). Mick is, and always has been, on top of things. If being a Rolling Stone is a job, holding the Stones together has been, down the decades, a sometimes exhausting, often exasperating but astonishingly profitable—and therefore thoroughly worthwhile—endeavor.

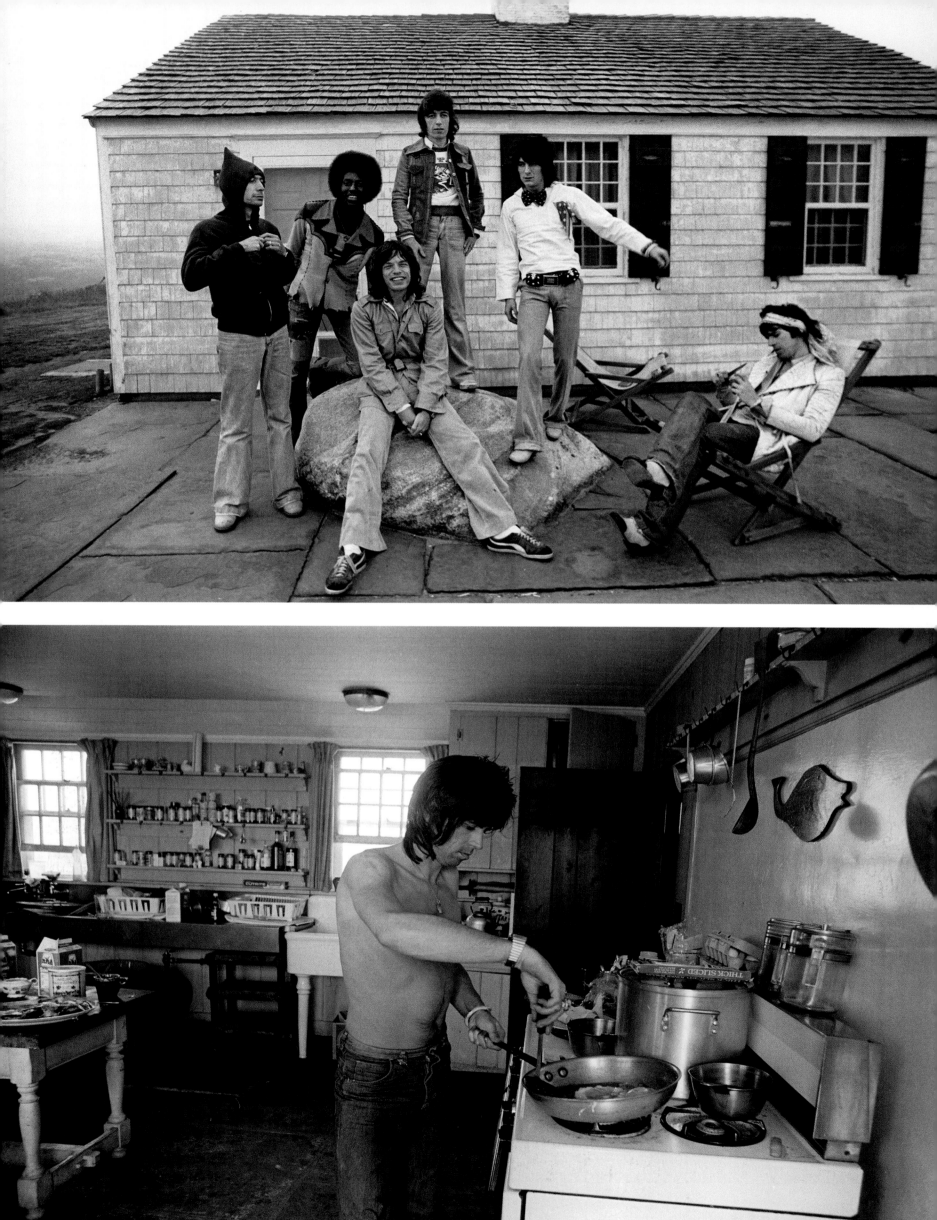

REJUVENATION: In 1975, Rolling Stones 4.0 (or whatever version, after the abrupt resignation of Mick Taylor) repairs to the oceanside redoubt of Bianca Jagger's great pal Andy Warhol. At Eothen, in Montauk on eastern Long Island, New York, the gang includes (opposite, top, from left) Charlie, sideman Ollie Brown, Mick, Bill, Ronnie and Keith. Bottom, Keith cooks some good, healthy food. The noted Ken Regan, a longtime friend of LIFE, was the one photographer on the scene and remembered in his book, *All Access,* "Once, I was sitting in one of the rooms and I smelled something cooking. I thought, God, that smells really good, like eggs or something. I went into the kitchen—this was still midday—and there was Keith standing over a frying pan at the stove, without a shirt on, cooking up some eggs. I had to do a triple take: he never got up much before six or seven p.m. Thank God I had my camera because this was a one-in-a-million shot." Above: Mick takes a vivifying walk near the sea. Again, from Regan: "On the beach, I had Mick Jagger all to myself; I roamed the dunes with just him and a camera, which was very cool." Below: All of this relaxation and nightly rehearsal is in preparation for the next tour and new recording sessions, already planned, as we see, which will introduce Ronnie as a Stone.

IN THE BAND'S recent history, Mick has proved ageless, as these photographs taken over the span of a quarter century prove. On this page, he salutes the crowd in 1978, and in that same year he shares the microphone with Linda Ronstadt (opposite, bottom left). The photograph at bottom right was made during a 1998 concert, and the one at top was taken during the 2002–03 Licks world tour. Remarkable.

KEITH (RIGHT) HAS, for 36 years now, had a new partner on guitar: Ronnie Wood, seen here on October 12, 1997, playing at Veterans Stadium in Philadelphia. Ronnie certainly has been a more simpatico mate than the difficult Brian Jones and the distant Mick Taylor, given to laughs like Keith is (and also, unfortunately, to substance abuse). He has fit right in with the Stones, just as he did with the rollicking Faces. It seems clear that he is in for the long haul.

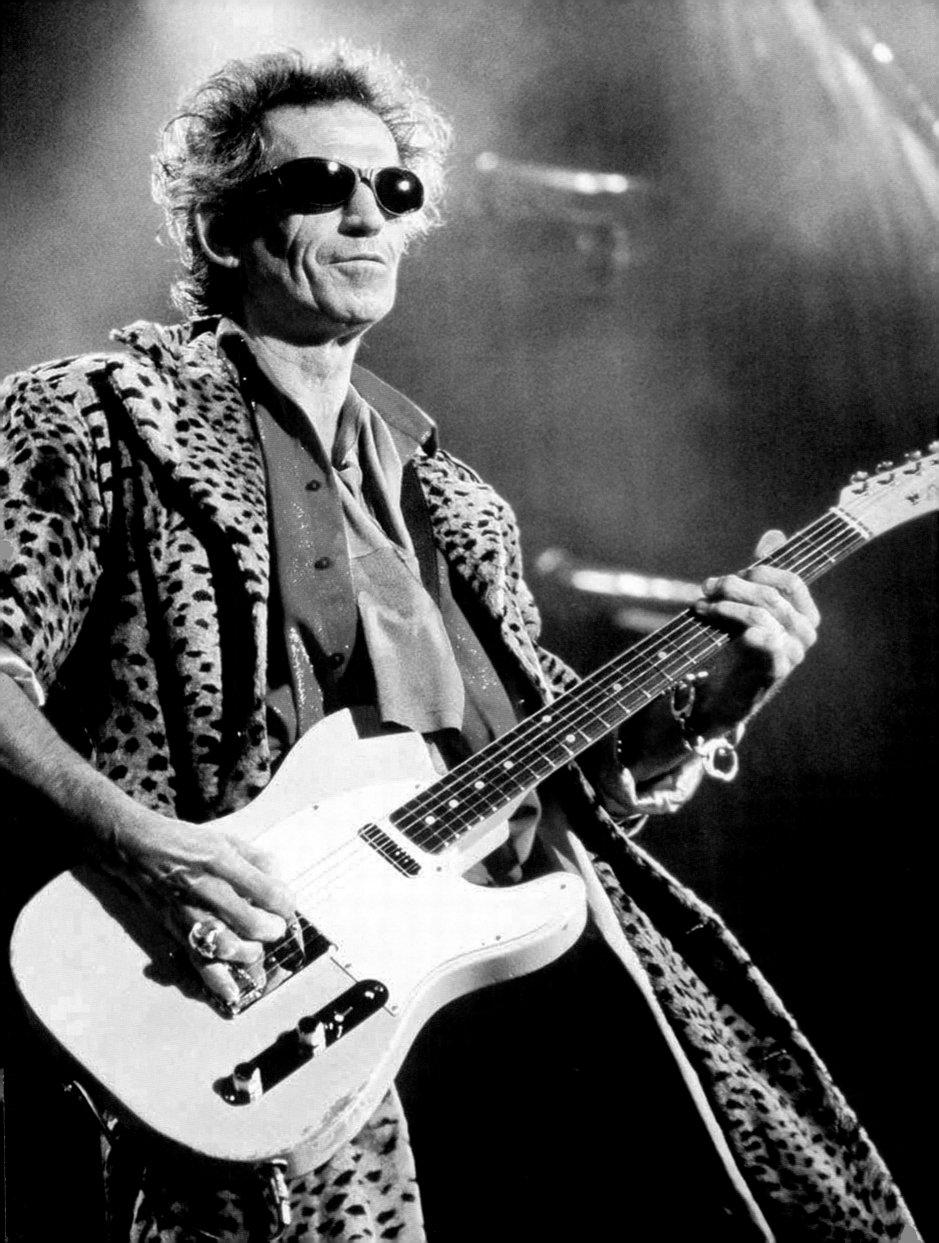

THESE PICTURES represent the Stones' dream, if it could have been articulated way back when—the dream realized. When Keith bumped into his childhood chum Mick in 1961, their bond was instantly rebuilt by the records Keith and Mick were carrying. Keith wrote to his aunt Patty at the time: "You know I was keen on Chuck Berry and I thought I was the only fan for miles but one mornin' on Dartford Stn. (that's so I don't have to write a long word like station) I was holding one of Chuck's records when a guy I knew at primary school 7-11 years y'know came up to me. He's got every record Chuck Berry ever made and all his mates have too, they are all rhythm and blues fans, real R&B I mean (not this Dinah Shore, Brook Benton crap) Jimmy Reed, Muddy Waters, Chuck, Howlin' Wolf, John Lee Hooker all the Chicago bluesmen real low-down stuff, marvelous." This marvelous stuff was to be the basis of their band—whatever band that might be. Did they ever imagine they might not only meet their heroes, but play with them, and even—goodness!—be accepted as near equals? During that first failed trip to America in 1964, there was one highlight: saying hello to Muddy Waters at Chess Records during a stop in Chicago. Five years later, Keith is clearly in awe (opposite) as he enjoys an audience with Chuck Berry himself: his all-time hero, with whom he has now traded licks several times through the years. At right he is with John Lee Hooker in 1991. Above, Mick greets reggae master Peter Tosh in 1978. The Stones' transcendent fame helped the careers of those they idolized. Their cover versions drew attention to the compositions of such as Waters and Hooker, and when Mick paired with Tosh on a cover of the Temptations' "Don't Look Back," this former member of Bob Marley's Wailers was instantly an international reggae star in his own right. Mick and Keith were respected and influential members of a fraternity they once dreamed of joining.

LYNN GOLDSMITH

JAY BLAKESBERG

MICK'S MILESTONES through the years have included many tours, many honors for his rock 'n' roll achievements, many relationships with many women and many kids. He met the six-foot-tall Texas-born model Jerry Hall in 1976, and in 1984 they celebrated the birth of their first of four children, Elizabeth (left and opposite, far right). Mick and Jerry sort of married in a nonbinding Hindu ceremony in 1990, and then emphatically split nine years later when Mick's paternity of a child, Lucas, by Brazilian model Luciana Morad, was proved beyond doubt. Opposite: On December 12, 2003, Sir Michael Jagger celebrates his knighthood with his father and two of his daughters (his eldest, Karis, left, was born in 1970; her mom, Marsha Hunt, was reportedly the inspiration for "Brown Sugar"). "I'm very happy, delighted," says Mick after Prince Charles dubs him. Other Stones are more skeptical. "Anybody else would be lynched," says Charlie. "Eighteen wives and 20 children and he's knighted, fantastic!" Keith's opinion of what he considers a "paltry honour": "I don't want to step out on stage with someone wearing a coronet and sporting the old ermine. It's not what the Stones is about, is it?" Mick's rejoinder: "I think he would like to get the same honor himself. It's like being given an ice cream—one gets one and they all want one."

AS FOR KEITH, the big day—without question—was December 18, 1983, which was both his 40th birthday and his first (and, we hope, last) wedding day. The marrying part was supposed to happen a bit earlier. Photographer Ken Regan, who was there, remembers traveling to Baja California, Mexico, despite his personal policy of never shooting babies, weddings or bar or bat mitzvahs. But travel he did, cameras packed, because Keith had asked. The musician was going to wed his love, the model Patti Hansen. But at the private beachfront hotel, Jane Rose, Keith's manager, told Regan: "We may have a problem with this weekend . . . It may just get postponed." Keith, in true rock star mode, had got it in his head that he couldn't get married until he had caught a great white shark, and after 10 days of trying in the Pacific, he was still without a nibble. Regan flew back to New York, only to be summoned south yet again a week later: Keith had actually hooked his fish. Everything proved worth the wait—as many of the best things in life do. There were perhaps 30 people at the wedding, with Mick (the only Stone present) serving as best man (above). Regan remembers about the photograph on the opposite page, top: "I have funny pictures of Keith and his dad, Bert Richards, in the bedroom getting a little bit stoned while getting dressed." Bottom: As Keith lovingly places a rock on Patti's finger, his famous skull ring steals the shot (as his mother, Doris, looks on). Right: Busting a characteristic Stones move during the reception. As the Stones reach their 50th anniversary in 2012, Keith and Patti home in on their 30th. They have two lovely daughters, and live principally in the affluent suburb of Weston, Connecticut. There, Keith enjoys noodling on his guitars, and reading. He confessed to *The Times* of London that his passion is books—he loves history— and that his hope for the future is to become a librarian.

ON OCTOBER 29 and November 1, 2006, the Stones perform two shows at the Beacon Theatre in New York to benefit the Clinton Foundation and also to generate footage for a Martin Scorsese rockumentary, *Shine a Light;* Bill and Hillary Clinton are not only present for the performances, but are seen hanging out at a sound check. The band—now, formally, a quartet: (from left) Mick, Ronnie, Keith and Charlie—has come a long, long way, and the boys are perfectly comfortable hobnobbing with royalty or leaders of the free world. A half century on, the Stones have ascended to the highest heights, and they endure. For how much longer this will continue is anyone's guess, just as it has been since that spring evening in 1962 when Mick and Keith showed up at the Bricklayers Arms, eager to audition for Brian and Stu, eager to form this thing that would become—that would be famous as—the Rolling Stones.

JUST ONE MORE

MURRAY THE "K" BRINGS TO CONN.

DIRECT FROM ENGLAND

FIRST TIMES in AMERICA

GREENWICH   TOWER BRIDGE

ENGLANDS
NEWEST
SENSATIONS !

PLUS THE

Chiffons
Younger Bros
The Epics

The ROLLING STONES

NEW HAVEN ARENA

One Show Only
7:30 P M

THURS
JUNE

18

Tickets: $2.00, 3.00, 4.00 - Reservations phone 562-3123

HERE'S A TRUE rarity, from the collection of Andrew Hawley: a Stones poster for a show that never happened, canceled, believe it or not, due to lack of interest and extremely low ticket sales. The 1964 New Haven gig didn't come off during the Stones' first U.S. tour, despite DJ Murray the K's sponsorship and entreaties, but they did play that Connecticut city (and this venue) the next year, and they thrilled fans at Toad's Place in New Haven on August 12, 1989, when they commandeered the club and delivered a surprise set that is still talked about today. The Stones have been on the scene so long, they inevitably come 'round and 'round again, and the stories pile up. Good for them.

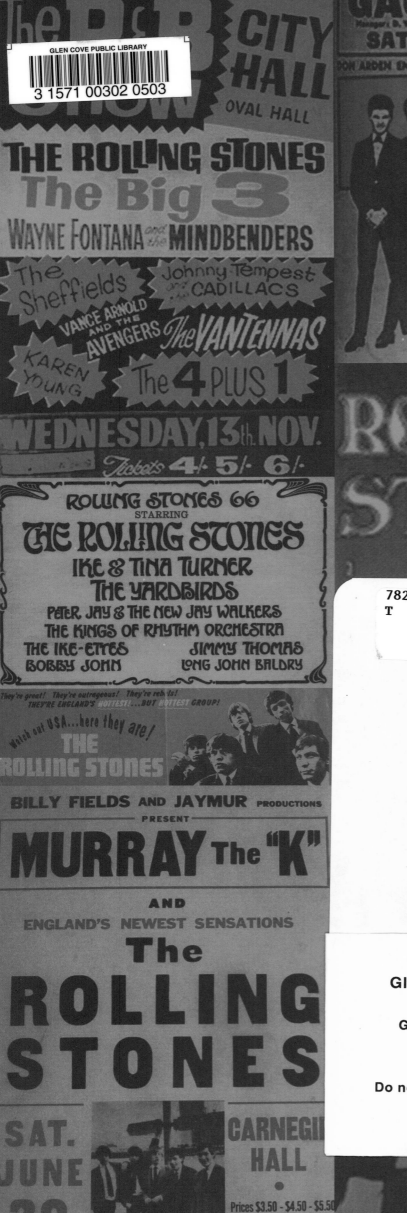